THE DECLARATION OF INDEPENDENCE

A TRUE BOOK

by

Patricia Ryon Quiri

Children's Press®
A Division of Scholastic Inc.

New York Toronto London Sydney Auckland
Mexico City New Delhi Hong Kong
Danbury, Connecticut

Reading Consultant
Linda Cornwell
Learning Resource Consultant
Indiana Department
of Education

For Sue Powell—my wonderful
Michigan friend with whom
I began my writing career
With love

July 4th in Washington, D.C.

Library of Congress Cataloging-in-Publication Data

Quiri, Patricia Ryon.
  The Declaration of Independence / by Patricia Ryon Quiri.
      p.   cm. — (A true book)
  Includes bibliographical references (p. 44) and index.
  Summary: Discusses the circumstances preceding and following the
writing of the Declaration of Independence and describes how it was written, approved, and announced.
    ISBN 0-516-20664-8 (lib. bdg.)   0-516-26430-3 (pbk.)
    1. United States. Declaration of Independence—Juvenile literature.
2. United States—Politics and government—1775-1783—Juvenile litera-
ture. [1. United States. Declaration of Independence. 2. United States—
Politics and government—1775-1783.] I. Title. II. Series
E221.Q58 1998
973.3'13—dc21   97-48966
                                                                      CIP
                                                                      AC

Contents

At first, life in the Jamestown Colony was harsh, and many people did not survive the winter. Then new settlers arrived, and the colony began to prosper.

A New Land

The United States of America is a young country. It is only about two centuries old. Europeans had explored North America for more than one hundred years before any settlers came to live here. In 1607, British settlers founded the colony of Jamestown, Virginia.

Over the years, more and more European settlers came to North America. They came for different reasons. Some hoped to find religious freedom. They didn't like their king in Europe telling them how to worship. Others came for the chance to own land. Still others came to teach Christianity to American Indians.

After the Jamestown settlement, the British colonists settled along the Atlantic coast. A British religious group called Pilgrims landed at Plymouth Rock in 1620. By 1691, this settlement became part of the Massachusetts Bay Colony. More people arrived, and many of them moved inland. In time, the colonies of Connecticut, Rhode Island, and New Hampshire were founded.

Over the years, other colonies formed. They were New York, New Jersey,

In 1783, all the American colonies were on the East Coast.

Pennsylvania, Delaware, Maryland, North Carolina, South Carolina, and Georgia.

In the beginning, it was hard for the colonists. They were in a new country where everything was strange to them. Some didn't know how to farm the land and were not used to wild animals. The climate was different and many of them died. But as the years went by, the colonies started to do well.

The Colonists Rebel

Most of the colonists worked very hard. For many years, they were happy with their lives. The land in North America was very good for farming. The fishing was good, too.

To show loyalty to their mother country, the colonies flew the British flag. They

An American ship flying
the British flag

were happy under Britain's
rule as long as the British government didn't bother them.

At times, the colonies
argued among themselves.
They disagreed about trade,

slaves, boundaries, and reli-
gion. Around 1763, the British
government decided it wanted
more control over the colonies.
For many years, British soldiers
had fought against the French
and the Indians over land in
North America. Now Britain
needed money to pay for that
war.

Britain forced the colonies to
pay taxes, or money, to the
British government. They put
taxes on many things, including
tea, sugar, and newspapers.

The colonists had to buy stamps like these to support the British army.

This made the colonists very angry. They weren't allowed to vote on these matters, so why should they have to pay taxes? Soon the people rebelled. The colonists who rebelled called themselves Patriots.

The Boston Tea Party in 1773

Many refused to pay taxes. In 1773, some colonists in Massachusetts dressed up like Indians, went on board British ships, and dumped 342 crates of tea into Boston Harbor. The action became known as the Boston Tea Party.

The First Continental Congress

Britain was furious at the behavior of the colonists. What right did they have to disobey British laws? Soon other colonies joined the Massachusetts Colony and rebelled against Britain. The colonies were beginning to unite.

George Washington (left) and other American leaders attend the First Continental Congress at Carpenters' Hall in Philadephia.

A meeting of the colonies was called. Representatives from all the colonies except Georgia met in Philadelphia in September 1774. The meeting was called the First Continental Congress.

The First Continental Congress decided to boycott, or refuse to buy, any British goods. It was also decided that the colonists would not sell any American goods to Britain. A list of their complaints was sent to George III, King of Great Britain. The list told him why the colonists were angry, but the young king paid no attention to the list.

The Battle Begins

On April 19, 1775, British soldiers stormed into Concord, Massachusetts. They planned to take guns and ammunition that belonged to the colonists. A silversmith and patriot named Paul Revere jumped on his horse. He rode all night and spread the word to other

Paul Revere's midnight ride in 1775

patriots. "The British are com-
ing!" he shouted. American
colonists known as minutemen
(because they could be ready
at a minute's notice) banded

Minutemen marching to battle. Many had little training as soldiers.

together. They were ready to fight the British if they had to.

British soldiers shot and killed eight minutemen in the nearby town of Lexington. This event was the beginning of the American Revolution

The Battle of Lexington during the Revolutionary War. The British are wearing red coats.

(1775–83), which is often called the Revolutionary War or the War for Independence.

Most of the men in the colonial army had no training. How could they ever win a war against Britain? A man from

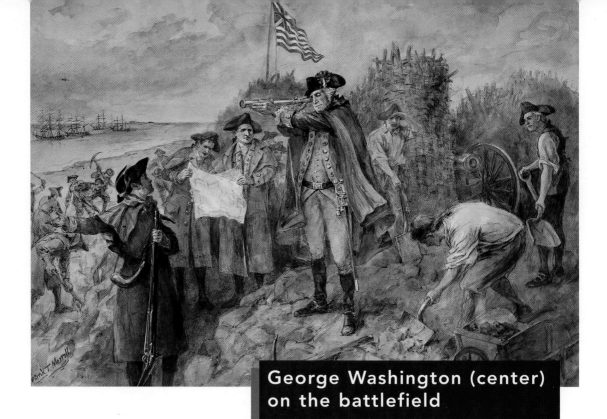

George Washington (center) on the battlefield

Virginia named George Washington took control of the colonial army. He was a true leader and trained his army well.

The Second Continental Congress met at the Pennsyl-

vania Statehouse in Philadelphia in May 1775. John
Hancock, Samuel Adams, John
Adams, Thomas Jefferson, and
Benjamin Franklin were among
the important people at that
meeting.

The men discussed breaking
away from Britain. Perhaps,
they said, the colonies should
become independent. If they
didn't, Britain would surely
punish them. Richard Henry
Lee of Virginia presented a

statement from the government of Virginia. It said, "Resolved, That these United colonies are, and of right ought to be, free and independent states . . ."

Congress talked about the statement for days. Seven of the thirteen colonies liked it and voted for it. But all thirteen colonies were needed to fight the British. The vote for independence was put off until July 1, 1776.

The Declaration Is Written

If all thirteen colonies voted for independence, the Continental Congress wanted to be prepared. Congress decided that a declaration, or official statement, had to be written. It would explain to the world why the colonies were joining together as the

United States of America and breaking away from Britain.

On June 11, 1776, Thomas Jefferson, Ben Franklin, John Adams, Roger Sherman, and Robert Livingston were chosen to work on the declaration. They talked about what it should say. Then they asked Thomas Jefferson to write it.

Thomas Jefferson was a skilled writer, and worked hard on the Declaration. Ben Franklin and John Adams

The writing of the Declaration of Independence

were very happy with it and made only a few changes.

Seventeen days later, on June 28, 1776, Thomas Jefferson presented the Declaration of

Independence to John Hancock, president of the Second Continental Congress.

On July 1 and 2, 1776, the Congress met again. All the colonies except New York voted for independence, and by mid-July, New York had also voted yes.

On July 3, 1776, the members of Congress studied Thomas Jefferson's Declaration of Independence, and made a few changes. The first

Presenting the newly written Declaration of Independence to the Continental Congress

part of the Declaration, called the Preamble, is the opening sentence. It tells why the colonies wanted to separate from Britain.

After the Preamble, the Declaration goes on to state that all men have certain rights. It says that all men are created equal and are born with rights that cannot be taken away. Among these rights are life, liberty, and the pursuit of happiness—the right to work toward happiness.

The Declaration describes the type of government the United States would have. It would be a government of

The manuscript of the
Declaration of Independence

leaders who were chosen by the people. The government would make sure that the people's rights were upheld. If the government needed to be changed, people had the right to change it.

The Declaration went on to state that the king of Great Britain had not given these rights to the colonists. A long list of how Britain had been unfair to the colonists was included.

The Declaration Is Approved

On July 4, 1776, Congress
met once again and continued
working on the Declaration.
Finally, the work was finished,
and Congress approved it.
That night, it was sent out to
a printer and messengers on
horseback carried copies to
all the states.

The reading of the Declaration of Independence at the State House in Philadelphia (below). On July 26, 1776, a Virginia newspaper printed the Declaration of Independence on its front page (right).

On July 8, 1776, people gathered at the Pennsylvania State House in Philadelphia to hear John Nixon, a Philadelphia leader, read the Declaration of Independence. The twenty-three-year-old bell at the top of the building rang out. After they heard the Declaration, the crowd cheered. All felt pride and happiness in their new nation. Once again the bell rang out.

The Liberty Bell

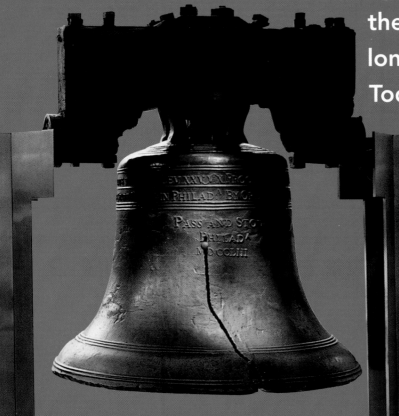

For seventy years, after the signing of the Declaration of Independence, the "Liberty Bell" rang out every Fourth of July. By 1848, a crack in the bell had grown so big that the bell could no longer be used. Today, visitors can view the Liberty Bell at the Independence National Historical Park, in Philadelphia.

The Declaration of Independence was written on parchment. Parchment is a strong kind of paper made from animal skin. Members of Congress signed the Declaration on August 2, 1776. John Hancock, president of the Congress, was the first to sign. His signature was very big. Today, when people say, "Put your John Hancock here," they are asking you to sign your name.

Molly Pitcher at the Battle of Monmouth. Women helped fight the long war for independence.

Fifty-six men signed the Declaration of Independence. The king of Britain was not happy. He called these people traitors and even said they could be hung if they were captured.

A Long War

The Americans fought a long battle against Britain. Although France helped the Americans, the war lasted several years. Finally, in September 1783, the Treaty of Paris was signed. The long war was over. At last Britain agreed that the United

States was a free and independent country.

George Washington, leader of the colonial army, was

elected the first president of the United States. John Adams was the second president. Thomas Jefferson, the author of the Declaration of Independence, was the third.

Jefferson's masterpiece will always be a symbol of freedom for the people of the United States. An original copy of it is on display at the National Archives building in Washington, D.C. The Declaration of Independence

The Declaration of Independence on display at the National Archives in Washington, D.C.

is more than 220 years old. It is cracked, and the writing has faded. However, many other copies have been made.

Celebrating American Independence

Since 1777, Americans have celebrated the birth of their country on July 4. July Fourth is a national holiday. All schools and most businesses are closed.

On that day, each person has his or her way of showing respect for the Declaration of Independence. Some try to bring history back to life. They dress in the costumes of the period when the Declaration was written. Others remember their ethnic heritage. Some just have fun.

To Find Out More

Here are some additional resources to help you learn more about the Declaration of Independence:

 **Books**

Fradin, Dennis. **The Thirteen Colonies.** Children's Press, 1988.

Nordstrom, Judy. **Concord and Lexington.** Dillon Press, 1993.

Quiri, Patricia Ryon. **The Bill of Rights.** Children's Press, 1998.

Quiri, Patricia Ryon. **The Constitution.** Children's Press, 1998.

Organizations and Online Sites

Bostonian Society
Old State House
206 Washington Street
Boston, MA 02109

Many exhibits relating to
the American Revolution

Carpenters' Hall
320 Chestnut Street
Philadelphia, PA 19106

Books and information on
the hall where the first
Continental Congress met

National Archives
700 Pennsylvania Ave. NW
Washington, DC 20408

The original document of
the Declaration of
Independence is on display.

**Benjamin Franklin:
Glimpses of the Man**
*http://www.fi.edu/franklin/
rotten.html*

Information about the life,
times, and words of
Benjamin Franklin

**The Declaration of
Independence**
Library of Congress
*http://lcweb.loc.gov/
exhibits/declara/declara1.
html*

A chronology and exhibi-
tion about the Declaration
of Independence

Liberty Bell Home Page
*www.ushistory.org/
http://libertybell/index.html*

Timeline, trivia, quotes,
photos, and history about
the Liberty Bell

**National Museum of
American History**
Smithsonian Institute
Washington, D.C. 20560
*http://www.si.edu/organi-
za/museums/nmah*

Take a virtual visit to life in
the United States 200 years
ago.

Important Words

ammunition bullets, gunpowder, and other materials used as weapons

boycott refuse to buy from

colony a settlement away from the mother country

declaration official statement

independent free and separate

loyalty faithfulness

minutemen colonists who were ready to fight at a minute's notice

parchment strong paper made of animal skin

patriots colonists who fought for freedom

preamble first part

rebel to go against

silversmith person who makes things out of silver

traitor one who goes against his country

Index

Meet the Author

Patricia Ryon Quiri lives in Palm Harbor, Florida, with her husband Bob and their three sons. She has an elementary education degree from Alfred University in upstate New York. Ms. Quiri currently teaches second grade in the Pinellas County School system. Other True Books by Ms. Quiri include *The Presidency, The Constitution, The Capitol, The Bill of Rights*, and *The Congress*, as well as a five-book series on American landmarks and symbols. Ms. Quiri has also written several books for Franklin Watts, including *The White House*.